@HOME on the HILL

Rindy O'Brien

Photography by Rindy O'Brien

First published in 2011 by

The O'Brien Group
www.rindyobrien.com

© Rindy O'Brien, 2011

ISBN 978-0-615-55759-5

Printed by Blurb
The O'Brien Group Publishing
1020 East Capitol Street, NE
Washington, DC, 20003

Photographer's Thoughts

Capitol Hill is a neighborhood that incorporates the history of our nation into its everyday life. Every street, a story. Every corner, a chance to connect with our past and explore our future.

This book illustrates the must-see spots and the tucked away places that make the Hill truly special. From the stunning historical Capitol columns to unexpected city graffiti, these photographs display the richness and vibrancy of a neighborhood brimming with life.

@ Home on the Hill is a collection of more than 50 unique scenes taken over a three-year period, 2009-2011. They reveal the Hill in all its wonder across all four seasons. I hope for those who join me in calling the Hill their home, this book will be a cause for celebration. And for those enjoying a visit to one of America's most fascinating neighborhoods, I hope the warmth and wonder of these images will make you feel just a little more @ Home on the Hill.

Rindy O'Brien

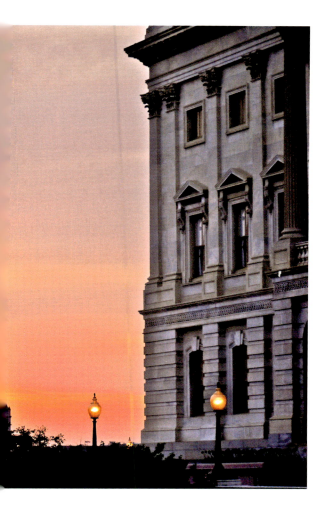

Capitol Lights

Star Spangled House

Capitol Grounds

Eastern Market

Catting Around

Mother Turtle

Sun Buggy

Vintage Deer

Just a Touch of Color

Madonna & Child

Lingering Lace

Vespers Prayer

At Rest

Cherry Harmony

Mondrian Moment

Bikers' Lane

Off Road

Walking the Line

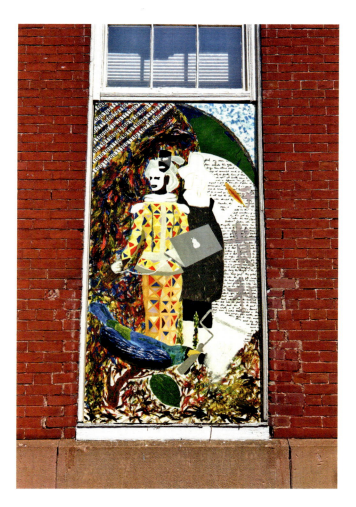

Love of Art

Jimmy T's

On Guard

Watchful Will

Paper Trail

Lunch Station

Afternoon Play

Big Wheels

Up in the Air

Hill Halloween

Blazing Red

Ghostly Surroundings

Elephant Walk

Yum Tree

Religion Pedlars

Thou Shalt Not

Ms. Seward

Ms. Bethune

"A" Alley

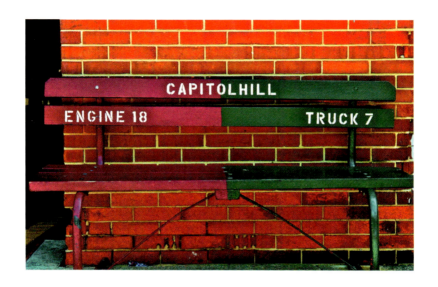

Engine Bench

Lion King

Garfield Pass

Capitol Columns

Asian Valley

Bonsai Garden

Marooned

Koi

Lotus Trio

Twilight Time

At Home

Acknowledgments

There are many to thank for helping me with this project.

First, a huge thank you to my husband, Frank, the love of my life who makes every moment a Kodak one for me.

My son, Corey, always ready to provide his awesome eye for good design, and more importantly keeps my spirits flying.

My brother, Curt, and sister-in-law, Lise, who suggested broadening the scope of the book and have provided critical reviews along the way.

Thanks to Gisele McAuliffe, a dear friend and colleague, for helping edit the book and photo selection.

And finally, to my pets, Maestro and now Lola. They have joined me on many of my adventures and have led me into alleyways, parks, and places I might not have found on my own.

Index of
Photographs &
Locations

Checkered Blue	419 D Street, SE
Capitol Sunrise	lst Street and Independence, SE
Graffiti	Garfield Park, 3rd and G Streets, SE
Capitol Lights	1st Street and Independence, SE
Star-Spangled House	6th Steet and Independence, SE
Capitol Grounds	lst Street and Independence, SE
Eastern Market	Eastern Market, 225 7th Street, SE
Catting Around	3rd and A Streets, SE
Mother Turtle	7th Street and Independence, SE
Sun Buggy	12th Street and Independence, SE
Vintage Deer	712 East Capitol Street, NE
Just a Touch of Color	11 9th Street, NE
Madonna & Child	St. Peter's Catholic Church, 313 2nd Street, SE
Lingering Lace	4th and Independence Avenue, SE
Vespers Prayer	St. Mark's Episcopal Church, 3rd and A Streets, SE
At Rest	Congressional Cemetery, 1801 E Street, SE

Cherry Harmony	10th Street and Independence, SE
Mondrian Moment	5th Street and Virginia Avenue Underpass, SE
Bikers' Lane	10th and East Capitol Streets, SE
Off Road	Corner A and 6th Streets, SE
Walking the Line	Hill Center, Fence, 921 Pennsylvania Avenue, SE
Love of Art	Capitol Hill Arts Workshop, 545 7th Street, SE
Jimmy T's	501 East Capitol Street, SE
On Guard	109 15th Street, SE
Watchful Will	Folger Shakespeare Library, 201 East Capitol Street, SE
Paper Trail	Eastern Market, 7th and C Streets, SE
Lunch Station	Union Station, 2/40 Massachusetts Avenue, NE
Afternoon Play	Eastern Market, 225 7th Street, SE
Big Wheels	Stanton Park, Maryland and Massachusetts Ave, SE
Up in the Air	7th Street and Independence, SE
Hill Halloween	308 A Street, NE

Blazing Red	US National Arboretum, 3501 New York Ave, NE
Ghostly Surroundings	Surroundings, 1023 East Capitol Street SE
Elephant Walk	Corner, 3rd and A Streets, SE
Yum Tree	12th Street and E Streets, SE
Peddlars	123 11th Street, SE
Thou Shalt Not	St. Mark's Episcopal Church, 3rd and A Streets, SE
Ms. Seward	6th Street and North Carolina Avenue, SE
Ms. Bethune	Lincoln Park, 11th Street and East Capitol Streets, NE
"A" Alley	2nd and A Streets, SE
Engine Bench	Barricks Row, 8th and Pennsylvania Avenue, SE
Lion King	123 15th Street, NE
Garfield Pass	3rd and G Streets, SE
Capitol Columns	US National Arboretum, 3501 New York Ave., NE
Asian Valley	US National Arboretum, 3501 New York Ave., NE
Bonsai Garden	US National Arboretum, 3501 New York Ave., NE

Marooned	Kenilworth Aquatic Gardens, 1550 Anacostia Avenue, NE
Koi	US National Arboretum, 3501 New York Avenue, NE
Aquatic Gardens	Kenilworth Park & Aquatic Gardens, 1550 Anacostia Avenue, NE
Twlight Time	US Botanic Garden, 100 Maryland Avenue, SW
Lotus Trio	Kenilworth Park & Aquatic Gardens, 1550 Anacostia Avenue, NE
At Home	9th Street and North Carolina Avenue, SE
Falling Leaves	Kenilworth Aquatic Gardens, 1550 Anacostia Avenue, NE

@ Home on the Hill cover art and design, Natalie Falk, NMO Design Company.

Photo Credit: Linda Wright - Artist Statement portrait

Special recognition to all the artists whose works appear in the public spaces.

About...

Rindy O'Brien has lived on Capitol Hill for three decades.

A native of Missouri, she came to Washington, DC as a young Senate aide and spent a career working with environment and conservation organizations to preserve wilderness, wild lands, and urban parks.

In 2006, she began as the garden writer and photographer for the Hill Rag, providing her a unique window into life on the hill.

Her photographic style captures life's chance moments and records objects and street scenes. She explores color, shapes, light, especially at twilight time. Her camera gives her a chance to observe and delight in the place she lives.